Paper Doll Fetus

Also by Cynthia Marie Hoffman

Sightseer

Paper Doll Fetus

Cynthia Marie Hoffman

POEMS

A Karen & Michael Braziller Book

PERSEA BOOKS / NEW YORK

Persea Books, Inc.
277 Broadway
New York, NY 10007

Library of Congress Cataloging-in-Publication Data
Hoffman, Cynthia Marie.
[Poems. Selections]
Paper doll fetus : poems / Cynthia Marie Hoffman.—First edition.
        pages ; cm
"A Karen & Michael Braziller book."
ISBN 978-0-89255-448-5 (original trade pbk. : alk. paper)
I. Title.
PS3608.O47765A6 2014
811'.6—dc23
                    2014026844

First edition
Printed in the United States of America
Designed by Rita Lascaro

CONTENTS

I

II

III

IV

I

The Phantom Pregnancy Speaks from the Belly of the Nun

Beyond the monastery walls there is a row of apple trees.
Was it the communion bread that woke me? In her mind
it was the seed of Christ. Beneath her robe a shirt woven from
horse hair scours her belly raw. Her want for a child was so great
it was the wolf's howl at the orchard's edge. Like a spirit
in a haunted room, I whirled inside her until the ceiling raised
and the woman loosed her belt. And then the days were quiet.
Many months I stayed with her there by the window, needle-
point in her lap. And as she worked, her hair shirt rustled me
to sleep. She has never known a man. Yet surely soon
the other brides who bring her tray of bread and butter
will gather at the door, wedding rings clinked to their
crosses as they raise a hand to their hearts, ringing the bells
of astonishment. Surely their eyes will be opened. The wolves
grow impatient in the yard. But in the evenings when we are alone
together, she gathers her woolen robe at her hips, slips her hand
to her belly beneath it, and there is a certain warmth I have grown
accustomed to and which stirs me, I would say, if I had a bone
in my body, to my very bones. I am ashamed, after all this time,
to slither away as I must and leave her deflated on the bed, her
wild eyes searching the room. Beyond the wall there is a row
of apple trees. She believes in me. It is good to be believed.

At Twenty Minutes Past Twelve by a Clock in the Queen's Apartment I Commenced to Give a Little Chloroform

—April 1853 casebook entry, Dr. John Snow

Snow, a name like a blizzard in springtime summoned to the Palace
where the baby turns inside the Queen. A magician's hand
come to release his apothecary jar into the darkened room
like a glass dove. Blessed handkerchief. Blessed sail laid at
your lips. Sweet drip of chloroform. What does a Queen see
in her closing eyes? Strolling the canal the length of the gardens.
Resting the fruit of the mulberry tree, heavy, vaguely womb-shaped,
in her hand. A name like white petals giggling in the whirl of his
swift gait, the glint of his waistcoat buttons all in a row, all things
delightful. Somewhere a curtained bed drifts downriver. Somewhere
a baby is crowning. Come back behind the closed door and lie down.
Come back already from the flank of trees. The bird has retired
to the sleeve. Someone lifts the baby His Royal Highness the Prince
like a balmy fruit plucked from the bed sheets. Has the sweet fire
thawed from your throat? Is that your baby? Did you see how he did it?

The Paper Doll Fetus Speaks to the Viable Twin in Utero

Days, a week, or two weeks passed before I discerned I was dying
and the things which were to be my eyes shriveled up like pricked balloons.
It is always night in here. I cannot know if it is you, though something
is wringing out my heart (what was to be my heart) my tongue my skin
is being ground to a pulp. There was not enough time to rehearse a graceful pose
before I was wedged against the wall. I am splayed like a weather vane.
Your head is enormous. When did it happen that I am no bigger than your footprint?
I am becoming a scrap of parchment on which is scrawled my flattened waxy face.
Unfold me. You will find a tiny skeleton stirred into the paper. I am a letter
to you, and it says if you held me up to the wind I would flutter away. At times
in the future you will feel that something has been lost but you will not remember
what it is. No one understands why this is happening. Look at me, you know me
better than anyone. I am not angry.

Poor Christina

If grief has no name then it is not grief. When I was very young
the casket was drawn into the sunroom. The light flushed its wooden

planks as if it were a dock, simple and orderly as any other, lengthening
toward infinity. My father's legs buoyed his body through the room

as flotsam through water. When my mother's blood
spilled, it was invisible. No mop was sufficient to collect it. They tried

to explain the sister I could have had but didn't. There was
a passageway inside my mother, what kind it was and where

it led I was not told, but if you held a straw to your eye
you could have seen my sister lodged inside. How did they know

it was a girl if she could fit inside a straw? Am I supposed to feel
sorry for her more than for my mother because she could not

come into the world, but what is the world? I was sent to live
on the farm. My grandmother was deaf. She never hugged me,

it was like she couldn't hear how to do it. The wheelbarrow
wobbled along clacking its cargo of garden tools, and the chickens

sank their talons into the crinkling hay. There was the sound
of cans in the kitchen chiming and the thunk of cans anchored

with beans. My mother's name was Violet and I could say it
as many times as I wanted. On the farm I got the scarlet fever

and the wind from the fields barreled into my room, the curtains
flapped at my arms rough as skirts of twine. My skin flaked, I was

a husk too long past harvest. The strawberry of my swollen tongue
shut tight inside my mouth. My grandmother's tiny body in the chair.

Poor child, poor scarletina. No one said that, I made it up.
And when I shut my eyes I saw my sister, the button

that undid our lives. It hurt my heart, the scarlet fever. All of it
hurt my heart. If your grief has no name then give it one.

Poor Christina, my father used to say. It was not
my mother's name. It was not my name.

I Would Not Offer to Disquiet Her

> ...with more strivings, but drew the child leasurely
>   with the crochet.
>   —Percivall Willughby (1596–1685)

By the time I was called for, the child
had lain too long in the womb parched
and drained of all humidity. I found
the woman's belly still as stone, ointments
placed on her body to cure the scent from the child
cracking inside her. Hastily I compelled her to take
a liquor of milk and pepper, and busied
the midwives with warming bricks in the fire
to place at the poor woman's feet. I bade her
close her eyes to sleep, and thus she set her head
upon the sheet but could not submit. The metal hook
warmed in my hand. I saw her eyes grow troubled
and I shut the door. In the dream I have of this moment
a ball of yarn is tangled deep inside the womb
and when I pull, pinned to the yarn comes a child's ear
like a wrinkled dress on a clothesline. And then
a pair of lips that ride the length of the thread
and into my hand like two birds perched upon a branch.
Like this I pull again, pull until I see I am stitching
a child into the air warm as a crocheted blanket, and when
it is finished I place it upon her bed, and she looks
upon the bundle wherein lies a tiny wrinkled foot-
print, proving theirs was once a moist union
in which for many months the child swam
and swallowed. And the mother is warmed
and sleeps. And the hook cools. And the mother lives.

The Flower from which Forgetfulness

Lie down beneath this tree this is the lying-in
velvety sweet this is the green sky dripping with
trumpets do you hear anything if you hear something
you will not remember it the insect that pricks your
arm flick it away you have much to do here do you
smell something lemony twilight the scent is narcotic
wipe the melody from your mind wipe the lemony
you may feel something but you will forget it don't
bother to scream just push do what the doctor
who is not here tells you to allow the invisible
nurses have you forgotten them already to touch you
these are the plants of the gods the hell's bells
the devil's weed push the baby comes in the grass
someone wraps her in a towel and hands
her to you now ah the trumpets swinging the angels
struggling to keep their lips to the stems, sleepy baby.

Two Beans in My Milk

At breakfast I said, "Mommie, would you put 2 beans in my milk
because I want to have a baby, now." I'm 3 yrs., 5 months old today.
        —September 29, 1942

It was my mother who said this, thirty-three years before I was born,
while her father lay in the sanatorium in his striped pajamas.
She presented the baby bunnies outside his window. He rose,
hauling his flooded lungs across the room. My mother
waved at the veranda, her hair radiant and blustery as mine
at that age. She had sat still the slow thirty miles to Stony Brook
with the basket balanced on her knees, the bundle covered in cloth
like warm breathing rolls, a braid of wicker arching through her palms.
Even as it met the glass, her father's face seemed to
recede into shadow. This was before the cat escaped the fence
and returned belly swollen. Before my grandmother drowned
all her kittens in the bathtub, wiped the splashes from the tiles
with the apron beneath her knees. By then it was getting hard
to find eggs and butter. Mother, I want to ask her
then, when she was still this girl, what will happen?
Before she braved her tiny fingers in the nest
and drew out an egg like a crisp new planet. Before her father took
the train home for good, grew fat on home-baked pies, and hacked
the chicken's head upon the tree stump where it lay like a figurine,
one orange eye sizzling. Before the war was over. When she was
a lonely girl. What happens now that I have eaten the beans?
The wooden ladle is in my hand, big as a bassinet. I am already
this old. My curls are still intact. My home is miles from any farm.
The rabbits that burrow beneath my deck do so in darkness.

The Lamb's-Wool Strap Speaks from the Gurney, 1915

I cannot guarantee no skin ripped from this woman's wrist, no
blood—it must be blood that stains me—I try to be soft, soft as I can
remember. Being lamb's wool, having once been a lamb, I remember
twilight laid out across the valley and all of us on the hill in its phosphor-
escence lit up, each kink of wool a filament of electricity.
It was quiet, just the buzzing in our coats, the hum of static
before darkness, just the grass crackling beneath the weight of our knees
kneeling into sleep. But this, this wailing my god how she wails, this is
neither twilight nor sleep. The nurses with their neat white hats sail-
boats circling the whale of her belly. She doesn't see them, though she tries
to spit at them. I take the feeble moist smack.
I remember birth on the hill, the slick thing slipping out, kicking
out of its dark sac. The mother standing, the lamb already standing.
No one came to take it away. It buried its muzzle at her belly. But here
it was days, wasn't it a day, before I hung loose, cooling
in the air free of wrenching wrist? Before she rose from the pillow, looked
around, before the thing was brought into the room, its hands flailing.
They laid it in her lap. She said Is it mine? She touched its face.
I remember it happened.

II

The Trial of Agnes Sampson, 1591

Aforesaid woman Agnes Sampson was witnessed
plunging a garden trowel into the grounds of the bone-
yard. A demon in the grasses, she was. Her crouching
shadow convulsed with each blow, a devil bird

pecking at the meat of the earth. She called forth
an enchantment, she raised a skeleton. I saw
her pop the caps off its knees and lop
its fingers and toes, and after that

the alleys rang their bells of echo
as her pockets clanked with human coin.
What hellish molestations must a pestle undergo
to grind the talc from bone? The wretched

crunching reached my ears as I was
kneeling at her window. In sorrow
thou shalt bring forth children.
Euphame was bogged down

with twin boys tossing in her belly. It is not for me
to say the way of sorcery by which a pouch of powdered
bone could drive the pains from child-
birth, but it is our duty to assert the word of God.

I knelt outside and listened for a cry or shriek. I know
her voice, Euphame's, shrill as a bird, but nothing
came. My knees were sopped straight through, so long
she lay in her delivery, the moss upon the cobble-

stones grew spongy with fog, and all of Edinburgh
slipped into a deep sleep. When silence
broke, it was a baby's cry that broke it. And
a second baby's cry. But

their mother, as I raised myself to see her in the bed,
simply cradled them and cooed a song
in rested, measured voice as gentle as a dove's. I submit
it here as proof. I saw the pouch beneath her bed,

and thus transgressions upon the Lord
aforesaid woman Agnes Sampson hath committed
and for which she will be taken to the Castle
of Edinburgh, tied to the stake

and strangled until she is dead, and a fire burned
until her bones are nothing more than scraps
on which is inscribed
the rightful suffering of women.

Testimony of the Imperfect Lamb

Soon as I'd slumped to earth, the sac around me burst
like the skin of a grape when the fruit inside is too much to bear.

And in a flash the world appeared. On the hillside, white corn
lilies, wet earth and a flock of ewes slopping though it.

The lily's leaves like a skirt that slips from the glassy
naked stalk and the stalk that throws its arms toward

the heavens and the fluffy bells fastened to the arms exalted
and the sound they make. And my mother's swirly fleece

is a map of the world awhirl with tiny cyclones. The wafery
bells crumpling in the ewe's lips. And the trees in the field.

And the snake in the grasses that betray its crafty slither.
How was I to know before now? The skeleton is essential,

every fiddly wedge. A throat to swallow with. A bellows
for my chest, and strength to squeeze it. In the time

before I blinked my first and only blink, I saw
that I would never last in the world. My mother's

tongue appeared and seemed to rasp across my face
and though it was the first, it was the best

thing my body felt. Forgive me.
I followed the instructions I was given.

The Aborted Fetus Lays Its Tiny Hand upon the Cheek of George Washington

(The coins and pencils are included as a size
reference and are part of the original photos.)
        —The Center for Bio-Ethical Reform

What does the tangle of blood say, the mangled
fairy shorn from its wings, what does it say? This is
the first and last sun flickering in the plaster sky.
At the window, a fly beats against the forbidden world.
The thing lies silent. Any squelch of its body on the tray
is the voice of the dispatching hook which is also mute
but for the human hand which prevails, master of the wrist
turning, and what a deafening wrench that is. Who says
a word in this room? A woman lies on the table in a paper
gown, still wearing her socks. Oh George the stillness
of its body embraces you, the silver wheel in which
the face of the compass turns. What now? The bones
in the hand translucent as fishing line. Holes for its nostrils
to smell you with. All the powder in your hair. The lights
go out. The fly drags the delicate hairs of its feet
across the glass a trail of sweaty little footprints.

One Child

In the year 1546, in Paris, a woman who was six months pregnant
gave birth to a child having two heads, two arms, and four legs,
which I opened; and I found inside it only one heart (which monster
is in my house and I keep it as an example of a monstrous thing),
as a result of which one can say that it is only one child.
        —*On Monsters and Marvels* (1573), Ambroise Paré

The child's mirrored halves
like the wings of a pale and cumbersome moth
splay upon the wood of the autopsy table,
its first and final tree. Is it true the human world
is too much for such creatures—a hand
swept across its fine hairs
cripples its flight forever? The body gives
to the scalpel what the scalpel takes. What does it care?
The child had managed its way into the world
and opened its many eyes only to be skewered by light,
opened its ears to the sound of two throats
screaming at once, its father's fist beating at the door.
The taste of its mother frothing
in its mouths. If the child had lived
beyond these few tormented minutes, what
thoughts could have pulsed in its brains?
What would it have seen, looking into its own eyes?
It is a marvelous monster that lies here, and
as such I plan to keep it and to pickle it in a jar
and exhibit it on a shelf where I pass
in the evenings. Floating
in dark waters shoulder to shoulder
as if they could be two children
forever looking upon the very room
where tonight my hands
nudge about inside them, exposing

their bright spines like two paths
converging, an arrow pointing undoubtedly,
conclusively, at me. And they will love me
with all of their heart.

The Stone in the Field Falls for the Goat's Placenta

It was evening when it first arrived. When I heard it
thump to earth, I thought it was another stone, a gift
come for me, a slick lump glazed with moonlight and

raspberry red. I thought to rally my round bones and
creak across the hill. I thought to smell her. Steamy. Sweet.
Pungent. Such an aroma not but in my fantasies. I did not

pay mind to the kid that jerked to life in the grasses swinging
its sopping ears, stomping dumbly at the ground,
nor the doe's teats. Though I saw all these things

I did not see them. No mind
the humdrum chugging forth of life, my love has come
at last! She shone as my own fleck of quartz

shines in the rain and which I call my heart. Thus
you understand my state when
the doe hoisted her drained body to her feet, the white

stubs at her forehead like a white devil's horns, and she
touched her nose to my lovely glowing thing. And then she
withdrew her nose bejeweled—a single dazzling droplet! I began

to suspect my stone was not a stone; its shimmer rubbed off
on anything that touched it, any foul thing. And then
she licked it, my heart wrenched, it unraveled like a lumpy rope.

I watched it dangling from her mouth and then it was
gone, it was gone. The little goat followed his mother.
She licked him with her horrible tongue. He stumbled, the

crack of his hoof on my forehead, I deserved it. I have
no throat to swallow with. Dunce that I am
I will still be a stone fastened to the earth.

The Homunculus Speaks from the
Bed of the Ovarian Dermoid Cyst

You can call me your little man if it helps when you think of me
I don't mind it. Few things I understand such as this
spherical mass which must be my head and I have attempted
an arm though my skeleton is only a crispy shell and I do not
know what it is reaching for there is nothing else here
but the moist bed I am curled upon. My tooth says
I might not look like much of a tooth but I was made
for chewing. My hair says brush me I am tangling
in the greasy spillage of the tissue I lie on
the tongue that speaks for me I ride it like a magic carpet
we are getting bigger and bigger I do not know where
we are going. I am trying to keep myself together. I am
not trying to be so ugly.

The Liver Speaks to the Ectopic Embryo

For many years you did not exist and then you appeared,
a pale speck towing your red moon by a string. I did not
have eyes before I saw you. I had not known magic
that could slip you from its dark pocket. How did you
get here? You touched me, you were delicate and tangled,
light as a ball of dust. Your moon collapsed against me
spilling its threads. It was nice to be touched, at first
it was nice to be touched. Months have passed
that you and I have ridden the unremitting night
clutching so I cannot say which part of me is me and which
is you. Your moon was a bulb I did not foresee
burrowing deep inside me nor its blooms unfolding.
I had not known what it was to be overrun. Ectopic.
Do you know what it means? It means you should go
back where you came from. When will the earth arrive?
It is always so close, but only you are getting bigger.
At times, a feeble light filters through the darkness.
Open your eyes. Is it the glare of the bright earth
impossible to get to from here? Do you know what it means?
Even though we are together, you will never not be lost.
I had not understood you were meant to leave,
but I must stay. You must stay with me
in these crowded heavens where the dismal planets
now are bumping against each other, and I cannot
say if I can carry you much longer. We are not,
after all, weightless.

Miscarriage

Your baby weighs as much as a paperclip. As an envelope
you forgot to seal the note inside. Your baby is the tip
of an eraser. Your baby is the water spilling past your palm.
The towel came out of the wash like new. The nightgown
you had been wearing came out with all its tiny
purple tulips still blooming. The room is scrubbed
clean as clean can be. Tomorrow, your friend is as far
along as you would be right now. Her baby is a plum.
But for now, your bed is trimmed with the scent of lemons.

The Native Lung

A young woman sits at the window. She sinks her hand into
a lump of clay and pulls a vase, lofty and wide, in which the air

can whirl about unchallenged. What in this world is not
but briefly in its proper place? The cat in his box

by the garden, blanket roughed by scraps of leaf
tacked to his paws. Faintly copper water

drips from her hands. The whir of the pottery wheel
is her song of continuance. Somewhere

beneath the earth a teenage boy sleeps in his bewildered casket.
The scar on his chest would still be visible if anyone could look

at him. The scar on the woman's chest can hardly keep unseen.
Doctors who want to open it up again. A husband who wants

to remind her he is not afraid. The cat who steals across it
like a border in the night. After a while, the vase

is strong enough to stand on its own. It is ready to receive
the roses she has shaped from beads of clay and now

thumbs to its side. There is a seat on wheels the woman uses
to push herself through the paths in the garden. The smallest

weeds release from the earth with a quiet puff. For all the air
around her, she cannot take enough of it in

to sustain a child of her own. The doctors draw
a cluster of pearls from her body. There is another woman

whose womb is an atrium, an airy ceiling, who waits
to receive them. What remains in her body that is hers? Even

the boy's lobe has collapsed and must come out again. What
remains? The fickle native lung. The vase carried to the car,

nested in a sturdy box. A husband to attend the fire in the kiln.
A tiffany lamp. A lent womb. A folded braid of knitting.

In the corner of the room, the silver tank waits,
the body of a tall, patient bird. A bird that would give her

even the air in its bones if she asked for it.

According to the Doctor in the Blue Gown, a Window

According to the doctor in the blue gown, a window is a part of your body that does not accept the anesthetic. A window is a breach in the peaceful house through which the knives blaze. You lie in the room beside the window where the red curtains flap, looking out, your skin bare. A window is how they drag her away with their hands like five-legged horses stampeding into the distant field. Only the baby goes through the window. You stay here. Close your eyes for a short dream in which you are sleeping, while the curtains are laced shut like an eye encouraged to forget what it has seen. There is a knock at the door. Your baby has arrived. How did she come from there? Look at her now for the first time, bewildered face tangled in her wind-whipped cloak.

The Infants in the Basin

Not until she fully drained her brood could a sheet
be draped upon her, she was so immense with child.
Linens make hissing noises being unfolded, smacking

noises being shaken out. Water boils on the fire. Both
make a racket with their sputtering—water and fire.
The floor and its din

roused by the nuns' slippers. Three-hundred
sixty-five bodies, none bigger than a mouse.
None could know their mother's

blood embroidering the cloth. A heap of
naked mice with human faces. The floor
shushed by the nuns' slippers. It is Good. A woman

can have an infinite number of children. It is Good
Friday of the year 1276. All the boys
are Jan, the girls Elisabeth, there is not more

time than that. Three or four go into our hands
at once. We dip them into the copper
basin. There are no cries or trembling,

no waking. The water
clasps their bodies and slips away. Beneath the sheet
the belly of the Countess Margaret

collapses. In the name of the Father
and of the Son and of the Holy Spirit. I have seen an ovary
excavated and a great many twinkling seeds inside.

He Abhors Not the Virgin's Womb

I say swaddling I say manger. I say Light of Light and you in darkness,
your little fingers curled tightly in your palms. They do not break
bread, do not know bread or fish. Your thumbs find their way
in the dark waters one at a time into your mouth, practicing
the suckling force by which the heavens tug a spirit from
an earthly body. What is honey and butter, what is wine?
Pa rum pum pum pum. The blood of Mary beneath your skin,
whipping swiftly about. What do you make
of the heralding that booms from the split-
open clouds, the angels' wings swishing at the skins of the
towering drum that is the night sky? Listen to it. Do you know yet
who you are? The flock and its shepherds a wide luminous shroud
gliding across the fields. The water rushes away from you, cold air
hits the crown of your head, prick of hay at your cheek.
I say verily, verily. In the hands of three tall shadows, something
glittering. What do you see with your new eyes, what of the voice
of the King? Hark! Oxen lowing. What will be your first Act?

So the Earth was Repopulated

In the days after the Great Flood, the earth wore a cloak of carcasses. Spirits were scattered about like jellyfish beached by the tide. The sun sizzled their delicate sheer forms, and by this they were made to stir and seek the dead and lie upon the hearts of the dead and the dead opened their ribs like swinging gates and the spirits returned to the darkness of their bodies. And by this the hearts of men were bolted back to life. Honey and bread were given into their arms. And on their very legs they walked and their robes swept the waters from the drowned fields and they found their homes. And once this was finished, minor creatures crept to life from wrung-out pelts. But the glimpse of death had seared their eyes. And it is as such today with frightened twitching bodies that vermin scatter the earth. Rarely do they touch men. But though it be strange wondrous from time to time in your nightclothes as you cross the room the two of you collide, the vermin stumbles and is gone but for a moment as its belly slides across your foot its racing heart shudders your bones and you remember.

The Calciferous Substance Speaks to the Sleeping Fetus

If you are going to sleep, then I will tell you a bedtime story.
You were too young to remember how you got here. There was

a long corridor and at the end, light, a warm room, a red dress-
ing gown already weaving its shape to receive you.

But there was a tear in the corridor, a ragged slit and darkness
beyond it. You slipped through—why would you do this?—the gown

held its form for a moment as if a body
vanished from its skins, it crumpled to the floor, the womb

snuffed its fire. You were too young to remember the darkness
was not empty, organs turned their

faces slick blind bulging and were surprised. This was when
you had no arms, no legs. Only a smooth seedling, what could you do?

You lay in the dark and unraveled a curl of shoots—clean, hopeful.
And when a fluttering sputtered up inside you, the sound of something

murmuring to life, everyone could hear it. For a long time
things went on this way—little heart, big heart—we grew tipsy

with the syncopation. You should have seen yourself dance. It was then
we knew you were all grown up. You looked, what was this

five-petaled whorl swaying in the night? The hand by which you knew yourself.
It was time for you to go. Time to put up the good fight turning, kicking, even

the big heart beat the battle drum. I'll never forget it, I saw
there was no way out, there was nothing I could do

but watch. And finally you saw it too and fell silent and still. And still,
I thought if you were going to stay, you would need a blanket.

I had only myself to make one of. I am not soft, I am
sorry. My particles rallied to lay themselves upon you

like stars snapping free from the sky
and everything white in this dark place

rushed to bind your shroud. And that was when you became my
white stone baby, my vaguely human figurine,

my little ballerina shy in her swan suit. Do not be afraid
if your arms are getting heavy, it is just the slumber taking hold, it's alright

if you want to sleep now. I will tell you a secret. No one will
ever break us apart. If we are very quiet. If we are very still.

Ultrasound

In the evening, I step out
into the street to watch
the clouds darken the end
of the sky, trying to listen
hard enough to conjure
you again. Today
was our first
meeting. Your ghostly
form breached the surface
a few short minutes,
white bones stirring
in dark waters, then
sank down again
out of sight. A rumbling
pulses through the long
corridor between houses.
What is the sound of
ultrasound? A robin
perched on our roof
like a figurehead at the prow
of a ship, the torch of her brick
orange breast, but where
are we headed? Today
all the dandelions have
released their seedling
puffs in one great un-
spoken current. They float
toward me now, one
after another, the
shimmering chain
of your spine, airy
by airy vertebra
they touch my arm only

the briefest touch, and roll
away. Baby,
take as long as you need.
The night grows dark.
The cottony seedlings
blow past, unravel
behind me
like a brittle thread. We
two are such a short time
together in this world.

No Midwives Can Do What Angels Can

—from the maxims of Cotton Mather, Boston, 1710

Wicked are her knuckles beating at your door. She sniffs out
your broken water, she summons a monster come tremoring

from your womb, she rides to your door on her broomstick, yes
she does. You are alone in the room. This is the inquisition

without a question. The fire burns until the stake is
whittled to a needle. Until the tongues are stilled. Shut your

ears to the knuckles' crack, you are not alone with the baby
coming. The dust now quickening at your skirts

marks the Angels' coming to your attendance. Sweet
perfume of feather, twist of luminous gold. Take

your place in the lap of Angels
which is your birth chair. When the time draws nigh, God

billows forth His apron to catch the baby easy
as an apple from the tree. You are not alone. The winged choir

to resound the Word of God. Blessed be
the women swinging from the gallows, the crook

in their necks that saves you. God gives only a perfect child
into your arms. The baby kicks. The baby cries.

Born to Give Us Second Birth

Nicodemus saith unto him, How can a man be born when he is old?
Can he enter the second time into his mother's womb, and be born?
　　　—John 3:4

The first time being born was not a golden gate.
Our skulls' plates wrenched. The air crashed
into our throats. So what is the miracle
of the second time? As old men, our backs return
to the hunch we practiced in the womb,
but aren't we just unrolled again
into the tomb? How then
to curl like unborn children? How
exactly does it work? There is
no sonogram that shows
the Spirit, whether marrow
whether vapor swaying, whether
waxy fold of wing. I believe in the invisible
Womb. The abiding Forceps of the Heavens
by which we are not made to bend
our stiffening bones. Where we are going
there are no skulls to wrench.
Not a spine in sight.

A Labor of Moles

At first sight of the World's Light, it commonly Yells and Shrieks fearfully;
and seeking for a lurking Hole, runs up and down like a little Daemon,
which indeed I took it for.
　　　—John Maubray, MD, 1724

On one such occasion I chanced to deliver a woman of a mole
as herein I describe this true and certain happening. The woman
was of the country. I entered from the gate where bees leapt forth
from the carcass of a small animal. And at the door a spoiled
mound of hay where countless squealing vermin bred, I saw
their naked tails swiveling about. And inside her chambers
the woman crouched upon a sour heap of rags. The fetus
inside her thrashed about so that I saw from across the room
her belly boiling. She was hard to still. I begged her push.
I readied my hand. And now I must report upon the midwife
who was taken of her post beside the open stove
which presently was coughing up a raucous spitting smoke.
And all the while the clouds were hurtling past the sun
so what I saw a moment in light the next was fraught with
shadow. A donkey brayed in the yard, whence upon a stillness
settled in the woman's belly and she looked to me with opened
lips as if to ask a question but the answer came too quick
the hairy beast shot forth from her legs, such speed
that in its flight it struck my knee and bowled me to the floor
I can attest I felt its pointed snout. I saw its stubby tail its claws
clacked along the floor it spun about I can attest. The woman
shut her legs and drew her toes from off the floor
as if to keep the loathsome thing from touching her. And
again I must report upon the midwife who presently was
calmly stepping forth and bending to the ground
as if to shoo a chicken from the roost, she clapped her hands
upon the Daemon and it wriggled there its paddle paws

flapping at the smoke through which she waved it I suppose
to douse its wickedness and then she tossed it in the stove
and shut the door. Indeed the Hand of God
thus spake. The smell of burning pelt flushed the air.
And thrice we knew the fire was requisite.

The Cesarean

There is no cliff you have ever seen icy or cold enough
to prepare you for the disquieting hulk of the hanging sheet

that barricades you from your body. As if you had fallen from
a great height and now must lie and stare at your own catastrophe.

You are alone in the room. The scalpel
lies quiet on the tray, splayed across a sheet of paper

like a fissure in the ice where the dark and silvery waters course.
In the waiting area, your husband stands at a soda machine, his body

dim as a strand of seaweed stretched in the moonlight, wavering.
He presses all the buttons one by one in the chance that a can

might roll into the receptacle, clean and shiny. Forty
scalpels. If there is a baby inside you, you cannot feel it.

The doctor is busy with someone else. There is a new language
of numb which your legs have learned and they are speaking it

now. Even your legs have left you. Only they two understand each other.
Your husband has seen the insides of soda machines before. A glimpse

here and there when the man had come to fill one up,
and each time he had felt embarrassed by the wide-open door,

the commingling naked cans. But
what is the mechanism that draws them out? He was never

able to see. When the doctor and his nurses shuffle
back into the room, your mouth opens and the cold rushes in

like a stone and takes the place of your tongue. The nurse is dipping
a sponge into a shallow pool. *Remember to bring my husband in*, the stone

is saying. The tray of ice drifts behind the sheet and
into the Inadmissible. Things happen faster than you had imagined.

Do you feel this? the doctor says. Your husband bends his knees,
has forgotten the coins in his pocket. The chill of the tile floor

stings his hands. None of the nurses have heard you. He looks
but the chute is eclipsed in shadow. The stone

in your mouth is not a bird and cannot sing. *You will feel
a pressure*, the doctor says, and you feel a pressure.

IV

The Embryological Sketch Speaks from the Page, 1874

He drew my eye. I saw a man crouching over me, a big hand
a delicate pen. I saw myself like a fish hook, wet ink glinting

in the candlelight. He started to tell me a story. There once
was a creature that looked like a fish hook and rolled across the earth.

And on its lance it nabbed the chronicles of our ancestors
and there were many pages yet to be written. Beside me lies my twin

who will become a rabbit. His twin will be a salamander
and his a calf and so on. I was told one of us would

weave a shell upon its back, but he would not tell which one.
Some of us eventually uncurled our arms. Thousands of years ago

I was told we crawled, we opened our mouths and out came
language. What happened next? He left me to cool in the night

and yes I shivered just a little. A mouse ticked along the wall
flicking the disks of its ears. The pen sank into its black well.

Come morning the man emerged from sleep, the dust
of dreams still clinging iridescent to his beard, and at that moment

anything was possible. His palm I thought by sleight of hand
had come to scoop me up, and we would step into the world

together. How does it end? His hand lowered the leather lid
that shut my coffin. And in time the scent of ink on his fingers

left me, and then there was only the scent of ink. And then a great
many faces opened me up to short reprieves of light, one by one

startled me by the glass pressed to their eyes. Their bony hands
rubbed their bony chins. Each time I looked for myself

as if through a window. If finally my tail were pleated with fins.
A beak sprung from my face. But even the glimmer

of the men's eyes was stifled by their squinting, anything
that could have been my form rubbed out by their shaking heads.

This page is a white net I cannot wriggle free from. I was lied to.
I never became anything. Dr. Haeckel, a book is not a womb.

The Ball of Human Cells Speaks to the Double Helix

I first awoke tingling, all of my cells popping in two, strings
of sugars and phosphors twirling to life inside me. I am
a cluster of gumballs in a glass balloon. The things
I know are small: my sugary middles, you like a drizzle of icing
spelling out your precise design. Each whirl of the script
deceives me. Tell me, will I become a daffodil and gaze
at the grasses through my yellow telescope? A fruit fly clutching
the hairs of a strawberry? Nothing makes sense to me now.
What about my long arms? What to do with my thumb?
And if I am a bundle of gumballs, then where is my sticky-
mouthed child? If I shook out your coils, counted
the times I could jump rope without tripping,
would that be the answer? If I strung you up like a ladder
bridge and climbed across. Surely I am not the child. And
if I am, then look around. Where is my gumball machine?

Prodigious Figure of a Child Having the Face of a Frog

—from *On Monsters and Marvels* (1573), Ambroise Paré

When the fever calls the sweat to roll
like glassy pinheads from their pins, lest your cheek

be seared by heat the needles do arouse, lest they stitch
you to your grave, it becomes necessary

to do as the neighbor woman says. Find a frog, the frog
that calls you to it by its singing, to keep in your hand

till it dies. Pluck it from the bush and fold its body
in your palm to which the jellies of its toes adhere. Keep it

steady through the field, returning to your pillow. The skin
of a frog is open as a loom loosely threaded, it receives

the fever just as a swatch of linen lifts the dew from your brow.
The room is quiet now. Sip from the glass with your

one free hand. Birds collect on the windowsill. The frog's
throat puffs and fills your palm and then retreats, a soft

heart beating. The day passes. The tongue savors
a flake of insect's wing still crumpled in its fold.

At sundown your husband carries in upon his fingers
the tang of the plow, with which the laces of your bodice

are now perfumed and now flick about your breasts still damp
with fever. Do not let go. How long does it take? Now the bats

zip past the door of night suspended in the room. Do not let
the frog impress upon your mind its humped body

too long in the dying. Whatever you imagine
shall be conceived. Hold it far from his embraces.

Concentrate. Your husband's face is right before your eyes.
The way a man moves, how can you think of anything else,

his face jerking in the shadows. Not the emerald
in your palm, no frog's lips on your mind. Not its

no ears. Not eyes engorged or tiny pits for nostrils. Think eye-
brows, jawbones, chin. Your husband's face

erasing itself. The frog slaps to the floor. What
have you done? The fever lifts. The child curling inside you.

The Softness of the Embryo, Ready like Soft Wax to Receive any Form

—from *On Monsters and Marvels* (1573), Ambroise Paré

At first, from the womb I saw everything you saw. I saw the papery scrap
float to the porch and looked, too, for the body of the moth
it was ripped from. Looked closer and saw that it was ash
when you saw it. I saw you put the broom aside, its stiff
blonde hairs. The neighbor's farm burning in the distance. You
walked to the fence holding your skirt, and I came with you.
The men already running from the well. Buckets
swept across the earth like heavy, low-flying birds. A woman
burst from the house with a gilded oval mirror in her arms
and in the mirror was the surface of a pond calm as glass
and in its depths a herd of cows snarled in a scarlet
seaweed. Beneath the oak tree, children
standing in a row. Couldn't you have turned away
when the barn began to creak? The horses threaded their necks
through windows wreathed in flame. Could you only clutch
the rail until a sliver of wood needled inside your palm?
When their lashes were plucked from their eyes, lips
torn away from their teeth. When the fire dissolved
the last gasping mouth of the animal. It was then I felt
my face burning. The walk home was black as night. In the evening
we went together to the washroom and my eyes were closed.
I had the sense that you had left me. The horse
appeared in your dreams, its human scream. Isn't
that right? My face burned. When I am
finally born, and the air is cold on my teeth
when the world is veiled in ash, and I have no lids
to blink the blindness away, how will I know you? At least
the whorls of your hair against my skin. At my cheek,
the chill of buttons I once saw your fingers flit about
before the mirror. Your palm where now the splinter
of wood is stitched for all to see. And they will
know by seeing it, you did this to me.

The Sound of the Maul that Cracked Open the Stone Child of Sens, 1582

> It was not until they had broken off a large portion
> of the covering shell, and seen the wonderful sight inside,
> that they understood what they were dealing with.
> —Jan Bondeson, *The Earliest Known Case of a Lithopaedion*

The sound was not an ax to a tree was not a knife to an oyster
big as a human skull not quite a skull sound. Madame Chatri
lies on the table her abdomen yawns at the world its graying
tangle of organs. But that is not the point. Two of our hands
steady the rock two hands swing the hammer. Make haste
twenty-eight years the tumor has waited to be born and finally
Madame Chatri has died. A cracking sound at last. The door is now
opened to the small room. Hair on the head I can see it. A tooth
in the jaw I can see it. Now here comes the iron extractor to wrench it
free. Off lops its right hand. Fetus! The hand to the wooden floor
thump what a sound. Oh prodigious delivery. Womb
of the dead woman. The rumors are true they are true.

The Protocol Speaks to the Mermaid Baby

You kick as if it were the sheet that made this white wave
you cannot break free from, but it is your own body
that binds your legs in a sleeve of skin. Sleek, cylindrical,
aquatic. The brittle thread that fastens your bones. This crib
is an island. There are some doctors who will take to the legs
with a knife, but they are not your doctors. Go ahead and wail
your song of sirenomelia. Do you want your legs split?
Do you want to walk? Do you know what walking is?
Where is your flowing golden hair? What will you do
with the third chamber of your heart? The emptiness
between your hips no one can fill with all its missing human
things. Open your eyes to the glare of the world. Your moist
amphibian eyes. You understand we must let you die. There is
little time and what has the world given you but flipper feet
so go ahead and flip. The incubator hums like a submarine.
Let's you and I make a pact. I will be the protocol and you will be
the mermaid baby. No one must be anything but what they are.

Some Thought They Heard a Rumbling in the Coffin

—from *Observations in Midwifery* (1650), Percivall Willughby

When no more breath came into her lungs
and she was peaceful at the pillow at last, the woman's
mouth was stopped with seed husks. The infant
still hung by its navel-string inside her
after six days of pains. Had the doctor's concoction
brought her only profound sleep at last, and deservedly so?
But not a moment was taken to witness the death pallor
veil her skin, nor moment to relieve the woman
of her soiled gowns and dress her for the ground
before the doctor, her husband, and the women
rolled her straight to coffin. The grasses
seized their footprints in the graveyard
as they scurried with the box rocking on their shoulders.
A woman soon returned to kneel upon the earth and heard
a sigh, the sigh of someone dying in the grave. Stirrings
trembled the newly settled dirt, the sound of a child
crying. We cannot say whether the mother woke
to feel his warmth upon her thighs, but
when they raised the coffin, her lips were found unfastened,
her fists full of husks. The child was tumbled to her knees
hand in mouth, having found no other sustenance
in the dark world shut tight upon his head. They both
were still. That night the coffin was left open to the breezes
and the townsmen of Ashburne came to look upon the woman
whose brow was silvery in the moonlight, the baby
with his finger hidden in his mouth. The grasses
were slow to regain their posture. Not everyone forgets.
And it is said the heat of their two bodies was so long in parting –
such was the friction stirred by their torments—that a steam
was caused to rise from them which shimmered and which,
despite themselves, all regarded most patiently till morning.

The Stork

When the stork fishes us out
from the marshes, we are just
opening our eyes to the cloud
of its body wobbling above us
half of it white half of it
black storm, its beak of black
rain stabbing into the waters.
What else could we remember?
The sound of its wings like
umbrellas snapping open
on the wind, the view
from our sling, the air
sliced open and wisping
past the belly of the bird,
whirling on the other side of flight.
The city comes like a barge
lumbering through the grasses.
Chimneys widen and sway
beneath us. The stork
knows the address, the fire-
place at which our mothers
stoop, her arms out-
stretched. Her pale hands
signal like a water lily
blooming in the depths.
When the beak
opens, the darkness takes
us, wipes our minds
with soot so there is
only the long fall, the
touch of human skin. Our
boundedness to earth. What
we remember.

ACKNOWLEDGMENTS

Grateful acknowledgment is made to the following journals in which these poems first appeared:

Another Chicago Magazine: "Some Thought They Heard a Rumbling in the Coffin"

Blackbird: "No Midwives Can Do What Angels Can," "The Ball of Human Cells Speaks to the Double Helix," "The Homunculus Speaks from the Bed of the Ovarian Dermoid Cyst," "The Lamb's-Wool Strap Speaks from the Gurney, 1915"

Connotation Press: An Online Artifact : "The Liver Speaks to the Ectopic Embryo," "The Sound of the Maul that Cracked Open the Stone Child of Sens, 1582,"

Fence: "The Paper Doll Fetus Speaks to the Viable Twin in Utero"

inter|rupture: "So the Earth was Repopulated"

Mid-American Review: "Miscarriage," "One Child," "Prodigious Figure of a Child Having the Face of a Frog," "The Native Lung," "The Phantom Pregnancy Speaks from the Belly of the Nun," "The Stone in the Field Falls for the Goat's Placenta," "Two Beans in My Milk," "Ultrasound"

Natural Bridge: "The Stork"

PANK Magazine: "He Abhors Not the Virgin's Womb," "The Trial of Agnes Sampson, 1591"

Pleiades: "A Labor of Moles," "Born to Give Us Second Birth," "I Would Not Offer to Disquiet Her," "The Cesarean," "The Flower from which Forgetfulness," "The Softness of the Embryo, Ready like Soft Wax to Receive any Form"

Spillway: "Poor Christina," "Testimony of the Imperfect Lamb," "The Aborted Fetus Lays its Tiny Hand upon the Cheek of George Washington"

The Harlequin: "The Embryological Sketch Speaks from the Page, 1874," "The Infants in the Basin," "The Protocol Speaks to the Mermaid Baby"

The Journal: "The Calciferous Substance Speaks to the Sleeping Fetus"

The Missouri Review Online: "At Twenty Minutes Past Twelve by a Clock in the Queen's Apartment, I Commenced to Give a Little Chloroform"

Unsplendid: "According to the Doctor in the Blue Gown, a Window"

With deep gratitude to the fellow poets and friends who read and critiqued these poems, with appreciation to Gabriel Fried and Persea Books, and with special acknowledgment to the Lexi Rudnitsky Poetry Project for its continuing support.